Twelve Dozen Four-by-Fours

Rhymes of a Cranky Old Conservative

T. W. Kriner

J & J Publishing

ISBN 978-0-9657245-5-5

COPYRIGHT © 2025, T. W. KRINER

PRODUCED IN THE UNITED STATES OF AMERICA

All rights reserved. No part of this book may be reproduced or transmitted in any form or by any means, electronic or mechanical, including photocopying, recording, or by any information storage and retrieval system without written permission from the author, except for the inclusion of brief quotations in a review.

Produced by:
J & J Publishing
P. O. Box 643
Buffalo, New York 14231

for Kim

You Democrats

You Democrats are sons of a bitch.
You've driven this country into a ditch.
You can't tell a penis from a vagina.
Why don't y'all migrate to China?

The Great Reset

Twelve billionaires want to call all the shots.
They'll be the *Haves*, and we'll be *Have Nots*.
My wife says they'll do it, and how can I doubt her?
I have a hard time resettin' my router.

Political Pharmaceutical Complex

Find a cure then push a disease.
It's what they do. It's as they please.
If they can somehow make you ill,
they'll do it, then sell you a Goddamned pill.

March Up Here

Our springs are bitter, cold, and wet.
I haven't seen a warm one yet.
And when the lion lamb departs,
that's when mosquito season starts.

Coyotes

My dog and the pack were birds of a feather.
In summer they frequently romped together.
The pack seemed to like him—at least not hate him—
till the foul winter night they suddenly ate him.

Mensans

There's a breed of men that need a label
that says they sit at the smart folks' table.
The truly smart folks have these geniuses beat.
After all, they charge each one for a seat.

Almost a Weathervane

A turkey crapped on my tool shed roof.
After a month I can still see the proof.
That turd is resistant to wind, rain, and sun.
If it isn't gone soon, gonna fetch me a gun.

Schiff

The man spews crap like a Canada goose.
With facts he always plays fast and loose.
His eyes bulge out like hardboiled eggs.
He's just another sphincter with legs.

Smokin'

Lola Astanova, Adrienne Barbeau,
Cote de Pablo, Brigitte Bardot.
Bevies of beauties have left their mark,
but none was hotter than Joan of Arc.

Open Border

Peggy Sue got buried. They put her in a hole.
The worms received her body. I hope God fetched her soul.
The "immigrant" who took her life
needs slowly peeled with a scaling knife.

Smog

The smog creeps in on little rat feet
and silently seeps into every last street.
It gawks at us as it sits on its ass.
Who knows how long before it'll pass?

Offshore Wind Turbines

When they're not falling down, they're killing the whales.
The clowns that promote them should be locked up in jails.
Messieurs Kerry and Gore would be a good start.
They've made spinning feces into an art.

Type II

Too many spuds and Frosted Wheaties.
Done give myself them diabetes.
My feet are burnin' and my eyesight's blurry.
If I keep this up, I'll be dead in a hurry.

Three Words

There is just a place. *Their* denotes possession.
They're is a contraction. Use them with discretion.
Add this to your set of mnemonic tools:
"*They're* all over *there* scratching *their* jewels."

Diversity Observation No. 1

You don't need to go to a big university
to learn what's to know all about this *diversity*.
It's really just one of the many tools
the communists use to manipulate fools.

Diversity Observation No. 2

When you want a house built and you want it built well,
you don't hire by color and you don't hire by smell.
You hire the best builder, 'cause you're the one payin'.
If you don't, then you're nuts. That's all that I'm sayin'.

Wish

As I watch the world's woes burgeon,
I wish I were a rocket surgeon.
I'd fix all manner of broken stuff,
then drink some Scotch when I'd done enough.

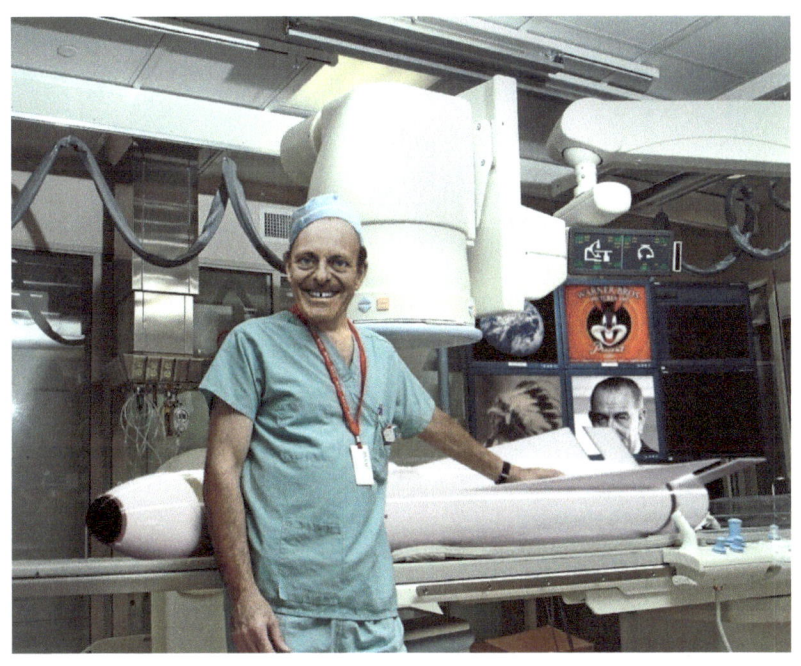

Marco Perkins

His mother was a lesbian, his dad a turkey baster.
He stayed at home with Mama till the government replaced her.
Now he's doing twenty down in good old Little Sandy.
Doesn't like that prison much, but his cellmate thinks he's dandy.

Useful Idiot

The man who gleefully feeds the beast
is often one who fears it least.
He does what he does because he's ambitious.
The beast will someday find him delicious.

The End of Yardmaster Hamza

He pushed his men hard when they worked in the rain.
He pushed them in sunshine, in snow, and in pain.
One fine autumn day, he pushed them too far.
They clubbed him to death in a cattle car.

My Heart

My heart is as black as blackest coal.
Somehow through the years I've kept control,
but lately it pounds like a drunk with a thirst.
And now I'm wondering who I'll kill first.

How German of Me

When misfortune falls hard upon someone you hate,
crack open a bottle and celebrate!
There's simply no reason to ever avoid a
chance to indulge in some cold *Schadenfreude*.

"Attacks on me ... are attacks on science."

Fauci's ego stacks up with Babel's Tower.
I suppose he's obsessed with fame and power.
He's a man of deep and bilious guile.
Well, at least he has an infectious smile.

Remembering Johnny Cue

He was a cross between a George Pal alien
and a shambling Dickens tatterdemalion.
I wonder how awful his life was, and why.
There but for the grace of God went I.

Splodge is Gone

He was a Brit I never met.
I knew him from the internet.
He died—I'm told he had a stroke.
I wish I could have met that bloke.

My Wife Expounds on the CPAP Machine

"I think you sound worse than you did before,
in the good old days when you used to snore.
Now that you sleep with that damned ventilator,
I feel more and more like I married Darth Vader."

Newsom

This guy is quite the proverbial tool.
He can't tell a piss puddle from a stool.
He's vain. He struts. His ego's huge.
And he's just another communist stooge.

Sissy Boy Attention Whore

He beat all the girls when he dressed as a chick
—and he had to make sure that they all saw his dick.
Now he spends all his days workin' out in the gym
'cause the Special Olympics are callin' to him.

Wild West Perspective

If you steal a man's car, you can ruin his life.
You might as well puncture his heart with a knife.
Carjackers should be summarily shot
or dragged to a lamppost and hung on the spot.

Remembering Kenny

I once knew a swabbie who'd sailed seven seas.
His massive beer belly hung down toward his knees.
His wife was a lush, but he always outdrank her
Till his liver keeled over and he finally dropped anchor.

To Aging Men

Your heart goes south and you'll get sicker.
You'll get prescriptions for your ticker.
The drugs you take will then torpedo
what little's left of your libido.

The Way of All Tattoos

Bob got his tat in '42.
It faded and blurred by the time he was through.
What started out as a regal bird
over time turned into a big blue turd.

Four Specimens of Stupid

Getting tattoos on your neck or your face.
Fist fighting over a parking space.
Paying for liquor instead of the rent.
Giving up fish fries on Fridays for Lent.

Four Specimens of Fundamental Wisdom

Hell hath no fury like left-leaning ladies.
An old F-150's worth five new Mercedes.
No decent beer has a twist-off cap.
Never stand up when you're takin' a crap.

Practical Intelligence

I've known some smart folks—doctors and such,
but only a handful impressed me much.
Those who reached for a hammer and saw
were the only ones who left me in awe.

Swing for the Bleachers

Early in life I was blessed with sane teachers.
Every last one told me, "Swing for the bleachers."
When you're faced with a task, you must give it your all.
Do a thing right or don't do it at all.

Deconstructing Yeats

"Turning and turning in the widening gyre"

makes me want to set my hair on fire.

There ain't no falconer. There ain't no bird.

The world's just one big orbitin' turd.

Archie Likes Parmesan Cheese Crisps

He's as fat as Burl Ives. He pukes everywhere.
When I go up to bed, he's sprawled on a stair.
He sleeps on my quilt (where he sheds all his fur).
Which brings us, at last, to my other cat. *Her*.

Harriets of the Gods

Some call 'em Karens, but I say they're Harriets,
drivin' around in their shiny Ford Lariats.
Whinin' and harpin' and havin' a cow,
thinkin' they're wholly holier than thou.

Bald

I've given up on growin' hair.
I shave my noggin. I don't care.
My head gets cold, but surely that's
the reason God invented hats.

Stevie Nicks Turned 75 Today

Her quavering voice is just so damned *wrong*.
Who let this woman yodel so long?
If she choked to death on a slab of Spam
I really don't think I'd give a damn.

F-1

This here truck ain't big on style,

but, man, it sure do make me smile.

Hauled me a gun safe, hauled me some wood.

Damn! This truck ain't nothin' but good.

Note to My Representative

You'd have us think that you're profound.
From where I sit, you just make sound,
like a yawnin' sphincter spewin' gas.
You're nothin' special. You're just an ass.

People In My Office

Linda skewered her man with a big kitchen knife.
Toni died at the hands of her son's creepy wife.
Vinnie robbed banks when he went out on break.
Barbara drank Drano, for Heaven's sake.

Cousin Ricky Left Early

At twenty-one he was just getting started,
when he sadly became the dearly departed.
Hit a deer on a hill in Pennsyltucky.
Neither he nor the deer was very lucky.

I, Polyglot

My seventh language, of course, is Pig Latin.
I learned it at school when I lived in Manhattan.
"It's easy to rhyme in that tongue," you might say.
To which I'd reply, "Uckfay ourselfyay."

Follow the Science!

The only science the Democrats know
is political science. Isn't that so?
When they smugly tell us to "follow the science,"
they're really just demanding compliance.

Undertaker

All of his clients are truly laid-back
and usually modestly decked out in black.
He thinks of them mostly as baggage or bricks,
as if he's a longshoreman down on the Styx.

Class of '72

I remember Melissa. She maintained a list
of all our dead classmates. Not many were missed.
So many names. And now hers is on it.
If I knew where to send it, I'd write her a sonnet.

I Could Have been an Engineer

Too much Suess, and not enough math.
I might have followed a finer path
if only my parents had kicked my ass
—and the schools had done more than let me pass.

Hope

I hope I don't get shingles in any tender places.
I know folks who've had it on their necks and on their faces,
and others who have had it on their shoulders and their butts.
I also hope I'm not the one who gets it on his nuts.

February

It's usually true that *you* fish the lake,
and it's safer than most of the drugs you take,
but sometimes the damned lake fishes *you*.
Then they find you downstream when the winter is through.

The Woman at Wegmans Staring at My Crotch

So pretty I damned near had a stroke.
She stared and stared, then finally spoke,
but she didn't say that for which I was hopin'.
She grinned and announced, "Your barn door's open."

Made in Heaven

A young Marine sergeant found the love of his life
in a Navy lieutenant he took as his wife.
They soon fraternized and issued a kid.
She entered the world half grunt and half squid.

When the Grid Goes Down and Food Runs Out

The orcs and the Morlocks will emerge from the city.
They'll show no mercy and have no pity.
You'll need your guns to mow them down
—and rest assured they'll come to town.

Grandson Jackson

This tiny Godzilla knocks over his toys
with a mischievous grin—like most little boys.
He spews strands of booger all over the place
from that twin-barreled snotgun poking out of his face.

Rusty Ford's New Gender

Face like a waffle iron. Strawberry nose.
Hairy and plump in his panty hose.
Says he's a girl now. Wears a dress!
Might as well claim to be Elliot Ness.

I Live in a Swamp

Well, just on the edge, to be precise.
The skeeters here aren't very nice.
Coyotes yodel all damned night.
Sometimes the moon shines clear and bright.

November Leaves

A gust of wind makes them seem alive.
They skitter and scrape across the drive,
like scarabs in a mummy flick.
The thought of winter makes me sick.

Via Paul's Second Epistle to the Thessalonians

On the river of life there's one thing you should know:
If you ride in the boat, y'all need to row.
Some words from the Good Book I'll gladly repeat:
If you ain't gonna work, you ain't gonna eat.

Reds

These commies ain't human—they're some lesser species,
with brains composed mainly of calcified feces.
If you meet such a creature, there's no need to pity it.
The thing will take pride in being an idiot.

Inflation

You get what you vote for—and I mean good and hard.
The clowns you elected should be feathered and tarred.
That buck in your pocket's worth less than a quarter.
The economy died by executive order.

Crystal Beach

I'll never forget the coaster named "Comet."
At the end of the thing was a huge pool of vomit.
The pool was so vast it had its own tides.
That monster was one of my favorite rides.

In the Driveway, March 14, Before Sunrise

It seemed to be damned near as cold as it gets.
My teeth clacked away like cheap castanets.
I smoked two Markets and sipped on my brew.
Went back in the house and nuked me some stew.

Along Cayuga Road

A sign I saw read, "Wicked Jeeps."
At first, the words gave me the creeps.
I thought the text said, "Wicked Jesus."
It's strange the thoughts that sometimes seize us.

Golden

Prevarications are lies of omission—
they're not half as bad as lies of commission.
But silence is better than lyin' at all
'cause you won't have to guess what will stick to the wall.

FDR Reflection

I guess I was an evil genius
because my thoughts were quite arsenious.
I might have poisoned tens of millions.
Instead, I locked up Jap civilians.

Ways Not to Go

Drinking drain cleaner or kerosene.
Using a pencil to puncture your spleen.
Drowning yourself in a men's room stall.
Crushing your skull with a bowling ball.

Uncle Leo

He drank like a swab with a liberty pass.
His breakfasts were Scotch with an egg in a glass.
He's somewhere in Hell now. Where else *could* he go?
Once he was handsome—now he's devilishly so.

To Militant Atheists

What's with you goons goin' after religion
like a jerk in the park who poisons a pigeon?
Let folks believe what they want to believe.
If you don't like the sermon, just get up and leave.

Rodent No. 2

They say if you get there first in force,
you'll likely win the battle. Of course.
But remember this, kids, as we've seen,
the second rat often gets the sardine.

We People on the Pavement

Can we coax George Soros and that lot
to kill themselves and start to rot?
To do as Richard Cory might
and blow their brains out one warm night?

Decapitation via Guillotine

One moment you're living; the next, you're dead.
It's simply what happens when it severs your head.
It's the cleverest method they've come upon yet.
It works. You can go ask Marie Antoinette.

Van Gogh

His ear swelled up, so he lopped it off.
The swelling was caused by folks who would scoff
and tell him to find a new line of work.
"Your paintings suck, *mon* silly jerk."

Rob's Departure

I guess it was his time to die.
He checked out in the MRI.
I know he didn't die of tedium.
It must have been the contrast medium.

Always the Duke

My dad would declare as he walked to the can
with a newspaper clenched in his massive right hand,
"*A man's got to do what a man's got to do.*
John Wayne said it, so it must be true."

An Old Man's P. M. BM

Sittin' on the throne, tryin' to launch a ship.
Dropped my Wranglers and let 'er rip.
My grunts and groans ain't cause for mirth.
This here BM's like givin' birth.

Proverb Revision No. 7

Give him a fish and he'll want one each day,
and he won't work a lick, no matter the pay.
But teach him to fish, and then fill him with beer,
and with luck, he will drown when he falls off the pier.

The Passing of Dick and Peter Piedmore

They got drunk and walked to the Bowery Station
where they picked a spot for urination.
They could have used a nearby pail.
Instead, they pissed on the damned third rail.

Covid Adieu

My old Uncle Eschol was on a mission
to succumb to a pre-existing condition.
So we made him get shots, but then just to spite us,
he died of blood clots and myocarditis.

Reflection

Sometimes your efforts aren't rewarded.
Sometimes your best-laid plans are thwarted.
Sometimes an effort's insufficient.
Sometimes a plan is just deficient.

The Peter Pithputtle Family

They lived in a shed near the railroad tracks,
and could scarcely afford to keep shirts on their backs.
Their meals were primarily stuff out of cans.
Their kids looked a bit like orangutans.

Bidenesque

I dropped my pants to scratch my crotch.
I thought no one was there to watch.
But I was wrong. The shame! The rage!
I scratched while I was still on stage.

Tinnitus

I've tried every "cure," but nothing will tame it.
I'd argue *Hell's Bells* is what we should name it.
Instead of this ringing that brings us to tears,
we ought to have music erupt from our rears.

Katie, Bar the Door

I'll leave you my 12-gauge. You know what it's for.
If the shit hits the fan, girlie, bar the door.
If the bastards get in, don't hesitate:
rack a round and ventilate.

Voracious at the Fridge

Breathes there the man who hasn't stood
in the kitchen and thought, *Is that pizza still good?*
If such there breathes, he's found his niche
—eating moldy mixed pastiche.

Huck Fochul

I'm headin' down to CheektaVegas
to hobnob with the local magus.
He needs to cast a spell for me
to stop that wench in Albany.

Curse

I hope your internal organs itch,
you good for nothing son of a bitch.
I hope your bowels unload on the floor
when you're standing in line at the grocery store.

I Met a Chattering Lesbian

She's half Amazon and half *Holy Cow*.
Her chest is huge. She licks her brow.
She's cloaked in tatts and riddled with rivets,
but she's smarter than many flibbertigibbets.

When Anne Boleyn Last Smiled

Henry VIII had a Groom of the Stool
to tend to His bottom with napkin and tool.
One day the Groom hurt Him with a pipe to vent gas,
and became the first Royal Pain in the Ass.

Points of View

"This really is not worth losing your life,"
was the motherly comment from my wife.
"Perhaps," I replied, "but *my* thinking is
it's damn well sure worth losing *his*."

Robot

It's one of many synonyms
for girls who look a lot like *hims*,
or *her* with that vagina hat,
or any other Democrat.

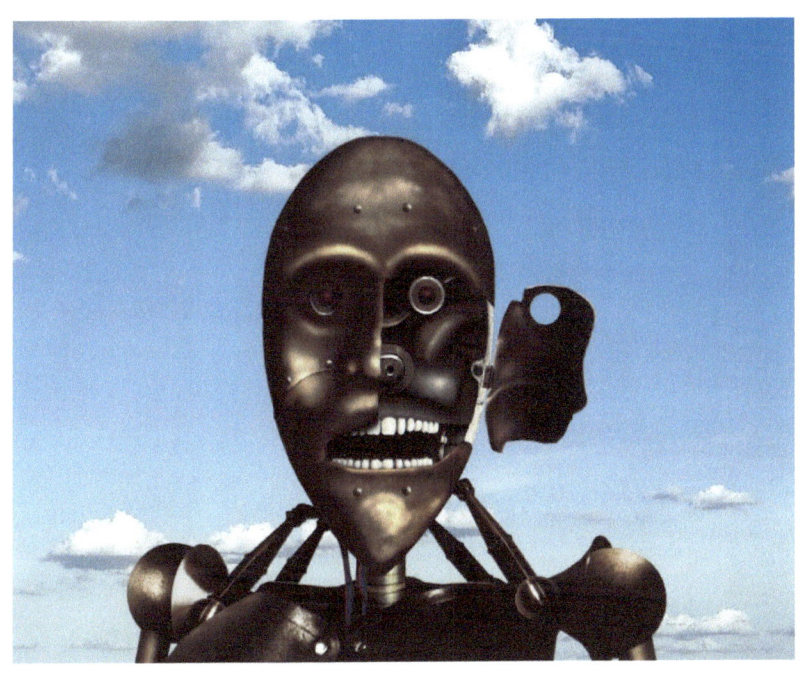

Your Dog

It barks and it yips and it craps in my yard,
then you don't clean it up. Is it really that hard?
I guess your little bag's just for show.
I'm saving up turds for *your* yard. Now you know.

Paper Mill Crane

It was eight tons of newsprint on a single reel,
a twenty-foot shaft turned from case-hardened steel,
that swung in its hooks and bashed poor old Eddy,
snapping his neck just like uncooked spaghetti.

Jen Von Chipmunk Killer

Armed with a smoke bomb at the end of their tunnel,
She lit it and shoved it in through a funnel.
Whacked 'em on exit: four 'munks and a mole.
I guess that makes her an ace in the hole.

Guy Monikers

The nicknames folks give you usually stick.
If you're baptized as Richard, you end up a Dick.
Sometimes you don't get one, and that's just as well.
It's better than being called *Mademoiselle*.

Up Canada Way

Math whiz lumberjack, born in a tent,
banged a drum wherever he went.
Looked for a gal to bang along with him.
Didn't find love, but found a logger rhythm.

How Uncle Miltie Went Out

He died as men do up in cold Buffalo.
His heart gave out while shovelin' snow.
He worked like Hell till he retired.
Then winter came, and he expired.

The Hanger at Home

He was good with cuttin', tapin', and mud.
Hangin' drywall was in his blood.
He finished himself with a 14-inch knife.
Slit both carotids. Left five kids and a wife.

I Killed a Bird with My Antenna

She flew straight in and showed no fear,
just a burst of feathers in my side view mirror.
She couldn't have done it if she'd tried,
but she damn done did it, and then she died.

The Handsome Soon-to-Be Dropout

Our lit teacher asked him to name two books.
The rest of us simply exchanged wide-eyed looks.
"*Moby Grape* and *The Dicks of Wrath.*"
He wasn't much better at science or math.

Gun Rule No. 1

Every gun's a loaded gun
—the fundamental rule, my son.
Those empty guns can kill, you see.
Ask Alec Baldwin or Brandon Lee.

Phoebe the Quaker Died this Morning

She squawked and she bit and laid eggs by the score.
Well, she won't be doing such things anymore.
Foul-tempered she was, but here's the thing:
that little green harridan bird could sing!

Back Hoe Operator

He carves the earth like most men cut cheese
—like an artist or athlete, with practiced ease.
He'll do this work for any fool
who wants an inground swimming pool.

Fatal Reflection

A jay bounced off my window and landed on the walk.
Its fragile neck was broken before the bird could squawk.
He'd headed for the trees reflected in the glass.
His flying days are over now. The impact killed his ass.

June 30th, 1:00 A. M.

There's a tree frog on the roof outside my bedroom window.
My joy to hear him trilling has grown a little thin, though.
He's perched along the gutter. I'd like to sit and watch,
but I've swallowed several IPA's and half a fifth of Scotch.

Looking for Woody

I know a lady carpenter who wants to nail a man. I'm not sure that she can do it, but she seems to have a plan. She made a list of things to do, and asked me to remind her to stop down at the hardware store to buy a good stud finder.

What Lies in Store

Comedic disaster will certainly happen.
I'll fall down the stairs or croak while I'm crappin',
or drown in the bathtub or choke on a spoon,
or die shovelin' snow by the light of the moon.

My Evolving Title

Hailed as a *prodigy* when I was young,
I advanced to *savant*, and my praises were sung.
Idiot savant was next on the list.
If they settle on *idiot*, I'll surely be pissed.

A Windbreaking Tip

One must be careful when one farts.
Sometimes the things erupt as sharts.
With this in mind, don't take the chance
unless you carry extra pants.

We Took Mom's Truck

Left my keys in Saratoga. Now my daughter's got to mail 'em.
If I had to take some memory tests, I'm pretty sure I'd fail 'em.
I also left my vapin' pen—can't put *that* in the mail.
The Feds would surely disapprove, and send us off to jail.

On the Road to Sedona

Tesla stopped up near Oak Creek.
At the wheel, Bob took a leak.
Pulled his six-gun. Filled a cup.
In the back, my girl threw up.

Progressive Fancy

I want to go where mice climb chairs
and unicorns don't put on airs,
where pigs can fly and dreams come true
—for me, of course, but not for you.

The Archie Problem

He doesn't even try to hide
that he drops his deuces over the side.
He litters the floor with little brown "rocks."
Damned feline stinks outside the box.

Last Request

A dying Scotsman asked his friend
to pour a fifth on his grave at the end.
The friend, a man of storied thirst,
said, "Aye. Do you mind if I drink it first?"

Grandpa K.

He recently rose from his box in the ground,
brushed himself off and looked all around.
"Say it ain't so," is all that he said
before heading back down to resume being dead.

The Girl with the Stupid Tattoos

A prettier girl you'll never meet,
vendin' corn dogs in the street.
Inked on one arm is Popeye the Sailor.
There on the other is Vlad the Impaler.

Mum Recalls

I once knew two sisters. Their last name was Tweed.
One was bow-legged, the other knock-kneed.
Each was as dumb as a barrel of rocks.
When they stood side-by-side, the Tweed girls spelled "ox".

The Matriarchy

Hell hath no fury like you know who,
but Heaven has its furies, too.
To ensure a long and painless life,
never, ever dispute your wife.

Daddy's Little Shadow

Helping my father was always hard,
in the garage, in the basement, or in the yard.
If I stood to the left or stood to the right,
he always barked, "You're in my light!"

A Niagara Guide for Someone You Loathe

Walk to Terrapin Point and pick a spot.
Jump into the rapids with all you've got.
If the fall doesn't kill you, you'll certainly drown.
Take a moment to fuck yourself on the way down.

The Demise of Howie Fell

Howie drove to Niagara Falls.
Girlfriend wouldn't take his calls.
Learned by text he'd just been dumped.
Walked to Prospect Point and jumped.

Late in the Day

I sit alone on my withered ass.
Time marches on. I watch it pass.
There's not much to do besides waiting to die.
That's better, I guess, than a stick in the eye.

Preparedness

Always have a backup beer,
in case you drop one there or here.
You must account for random spilling
before you go to your man cave for swilling.

The Old Man and the Pee

The pressure grows until it hurts.
Then all that comes out is a couple of squirts.
Four times each night the fluid wakes him,
and will until the Good Lord takes him.

Rushing by Woods on a Sultry Evening

Whose woods these are I just don't care.
He could live damned near anywhere.
I only know they're filled with skeeters
that want to drain my blood by liters.

Egress of the Ogress

She was anything but a kindly Samaritan
—a communist crone best described as a harridan.
She clawed through our lives as a strident virago,
and now that she's dead, she can vote in Chicago.

Point of Grammar

Take *number*, for instance, there's *fewer* and *less*.
Which word to employ is often a guess.
When countin' out turds, if you flush one, you've *fewer*.
Failure to flush means *less* crap in the sewer.

A Second Point of Grammar

Amount and *number* are sure to confuse.
Media folks don't know which one to use.
It's *number* of people. It isn't *amount*—
that word is reserved for stuff you can't count.

Prometheus

He stole beer from his folks. We drank it.
He took his grandpa's boat. We sank it.
He went to prison and got raped.
I'm not sure how, but I escaped.

Denouement

I've had many questions about faith versus knowledge
that didn't get answered in church or at college.
I guess when I die I'll find out what's in store.
Then I'll get all my answers or won't ask anymore.

Mum's Credo

You're near alone in the universe
till they haul you off in a big black hearse.
When troubles come, they come by twelves.
The Lord helps those who help themselves.

Dale Memory No. 3

He could always drum up a room-clearing fart.
He called it a science. I think it was art.
He'd lift his foot and pump his leg.
And soon we'd smell a rotten egg.

Inground Pool

Skeeters, snakes, spiders, 'munks,
the neighbor's dog, some rabid skunks.
They come to my house for their swimmin',
but they never bring no pretty women.

The Incomparable Al Gore

Here's an inconvenient truth:
Al lost out in the voting booth,
but despite being damned near as dumb as a hammer
he made loads of cash as a climate change scammer.

Massage Therapy Fail

My quarrelsome friend planned to be a masseur,
but his chosen career ended up in the sewer.
He failed, of course, I'm sorry to say.
He just rubbed folks the wrong damned way.

The Selection Process

Pilsner, lager, or IPA.
Which of these shall I drink today?
As long as it's brewed and can flow from a tap,
I guess I really don't give a crap.

Feline Propensity

If you buy a sandbox for your kid,
make sure you get one with a lid.
If not, the cats from far and wide
will leave their little gifts inside.

Altitude

A mouse in my garage refuses to die.
I want that little bastard to fry.
He chews through my canvas and craps everywhere.
And I'll kill him—once I get down from this chair.

Skeeters

Early in spring they emerge from the swamp
and begin their annual bloodthirsty romp.
Nothing annoys like the close buzzing sound
of these tiny phlebotomists flying around.

Grandpa C.

My mother's father would sometimes say,
"If you don't drink or smoke or nibble on hay,
you're nothing more than a wannabe priest,
and not fit company for man or beast."

Chicago Wish

If I had a single wish,
Chicago's king would be a fish.
He'd rule the place with an iron fin,
so losers there would sometimes win.

Seasonal Bitch

In wintertime we curse the snow—
it's what we do in Buffalo.
Now in summer, it's so damned hot,
we miss the snow we haven't got.

Hunter's Pardon

He should be locked in a penitentiary
for being the Big Guy's plenipotentiary.
Instead, he'll continue his life of ease,
snorting cocaine and learning Chinese.

An Abbreviated Ode to Julie Andrews

Chihuahuas and geeks with a penchant for dancing.
Martial arts movies and Gothic romancing.
Men dressed as women who can't menstruate
—these are a few of the things that I hate.

Earned Income Tax credits, gun control lobbies.
Illegal alien activist hobbies.
FBI agents who kick down my door
—these are a few of the things I abhor.

When the sun shines, when life seems great,
I don't knock on wood.
I simply remember the things that I hate
and then I don't feel so good.

Antifa and MENSA and Emily's List,
and most of the women that I've ever kissed.
Melanin Scholars and men with bow-ties
—these are a few of the things I despise.

About the Illustrations

The images in this book are manipulations of photographs from the author's collection and from public domain or free images obtained fromPixabay.com, UnSplash.com, Morguefile.com, commons.wikimedia.org, and the U. S. Government.

About the Author

T. W. Kriner lives in a New York swamp with his wife and two cats.

www.ingramcontent.com/pod-product-compliance
Lightning Source LLC
Chambersburg PA
CBHW042336150426
43195CB00001B/6